Copyright © 2021 All rights reserved.

The content contained within this book may not be reproduced, duplicated, or transmitted without direct written permission from the author or the publisher. Under no circumstances will any blame or legal responsibility be held against the publisher, or author, for any damages, reparation, or monetary loss due to the information contained within this book, either directly or indirectly.

Legal Notice: This book is copyright protected. It is only for personal use. You cannot amend, distribute, sell, use, quote or paraphrase any part, or the content within this book, without the consent of the author or publisher.

Disclaimer Notice: Please note the information contained within this document is for educational and entertainment purposes only. All effort has been executed to present accurate, up to date, reliable, complete information. No warranties of any kind are declared or implied. Readers acknowledge that the author is not engaged in the rendering of legal, financial, medical, or professional advice. The content within this book has been derived from various sources. Please consult a licensed professional before attempting any techniques outlined in this book. By reading this document, the reader agrees that under no circumstances is the author responsible for any losses, direct or indirect, that are incurred as a result of the use of the information contained within this document, including, but not limited to, errors, omissions, or inaccuracies.

CONTENTS

INTRODUCTION 5

PART1: SMOOTHIE BASICS 6

PART 2: TROPICAL SMOOTHIES 10

    Pineapple & Mango With Orange 10

    Triple Melon Shake With Mint 11

    Banana & Date Shake With Walnuts 12

    Watermelon Cooler With Mixed Berries 13

    Mango Madness With Banana & Vanilla 14

    Gingersnap Crunch With Bananas & Honey 15

    Kiwi & Orange Burst With Strawberries 16

    Shooting Star Fruit With Peaches & Coconut 17

    Goji Berries & Bananas With Coconut 18

    Dragon Fruit Dream With Raspberries & Honey 19

    Pom Pom With Clementine 20

    Pineapple Mojito With Lime & Mint 21

    Guava & Mango Lassi With Chia Seeds & Coconut 22

    Pineapple & Coconut With Banana & Honey 23

    Banana & Mango Pops With Coconut & Honey 24

    Blood Orange Margarita With Peaches & Key Lime 25

    Açaí & Pineapple Bowl With Chia Seeds & Walnuts 26

    Coconut Quartet With Lime 27

    Grapefruit Detox With Green Tea & Beet 28

    Lychee & Lemon With Coconut 29

    Roasted Pineapple With Cottage Cheese 30

    Pineapple & Spinach With Cilantro & Ginger 31

    Açaí & Peach Bowl With Pineapple & Orange 32

    Passion Fruit With Orange & Banana 33

    Papaya & Honey With Flaxseed 34

PART 3: BERRY SMOOTHIES 35

    Wild Blueberry Blast With Banana & Chia Seeds 35

    Oats & Strawberries With Blueberries 36

    Blackberries & Banana With Coconut 37

    Chocolate & Cherries With a Pinch Of Sea Salt 38

Raspberry Creamsicles With Banana & Honey 39
Nectarine Tubes With Blackberries 40
Raspberry Brûlée With Cream Cheese 41
Red Currants & Honey With Banana & Coconut 42
Blueberry Cheesecake With Banana & Vanilla 43
Mixed Berry Crunch With a Touch Of Honey 44
Raspberries & Chia Seeds With a Hint Of Maple 45
Strawberry Delight With Rhubarb & Honey 46
Strawberries & Vanilla With Lavender 47
Roasted Grapes With Banana 48
Strawberry Sundae With Banana 49
Fruit Salad Surprise With Coconut & Chia Seeds 50
Pb & J Shake With Banana & Oats 51
Three-Layer Berry Treat With Apple & Honey 52
Cranberry Rejuvenator With Orange 53
Mixed Berries & Beet With Banana & Lemon 54
Strawberries & Pineapple With Orange 55
Mixed Berry Shock With Beet 56
Tart Cherry Shake With Vanilla 57
Strawberries & Hemp With a Hint Of Maple 58
Backyard Berries With Vanilla Frozen Yogurt 59

PART 4: COMBO SMOOTHIES 60
Carrots & Apples With a Splash Of Lemon 60
Pumpkin Pie With Maple & Flaxseed 61
Chocolate Shake With Cauliflower 62
Golden Butternut With a Touch Of Honey 63
Pineapple & Chia Bowl With Banana & Orange 64
Tomatoes & Basil With a Splash Of Lemon 65
Peanut Butter Shake With Cottage Cheese 66
Pumpkin Power With Banana & Maple 67
Apricot Horchata With Cinnamon 68
Cashews & Kale With Banana & Maple 69
Turmeric Latte With Bananas & Maple 70
Homemade Almond Milk With Bananas & Vanilla 71
Lentils & Peanut Butter With Banana 72
Creamy Cauliflower With Banana & Almond 73
Dandy Watermelon With Apple 74
Carrots & Chai With Mango 75

Sweet Potato Shake With Orange & Ginger...76
Vanilla Kefir With Lime...77
Celery & Cayenne With Lemon..78
Chocolate Cold Brew With Coffee & Mint..79
Spinach & Pears With Lemon...80
Coconut & Edamame With a Touch Of Honey..81
Cucumber Chiller With Honeydew..82
Fig & Almond Bowl With Bananas..83
Plum & Jicama With Cashews & Honey...84
Sweet Potato Bowl With Cantaloupe...85
Peachy Green Tea With Honey & Ginger...86
Virgin Bloody Mary With Celery & Lemon..87
Lemon & Beet With a Touch Of Honey..88
Pumpkin & Maple With Banana & Cinnamon..89

PART 5: GREEN SMOOTHIES **90**
Sweet Pea Shake With Pineapple & Lime...90
Spinach & Banana With Chia Seeds & Green Tea...91
Clementine & Banana With Wheatgrass & Coconut...92
Matcha Latte With Banana & Honey...93
Kale Lemonade With a Touch Of Honey..94
Avocado & Cilantro With a Splash Of Lime...95
Key Lime & Romaine With Coconut & Banana...96
Ultimate Kombucha With Spinach..97
Cucumber Shakeup With Lime..98
Kale & Green Apple With Ginger..99
Tomatillo Whirl With Honey & Lime..100
Mango Pops With Dates & Spinach...101
Spinach & Bananas With Dates..102
Avocado Bliss With Coconut & Banana..103
Spinach & Apple With Broccoli & Banana..104
Avocado & Kiwi With Mint..105
Pineapple & Parsley With Spinach & Banana..106
Ginger Detox With Pineapple...107
Zucchini Blast With Bok Choy & Lemon..108
Kale Chiller With Lemon...109

INTRODUCTION

Getting Fresh

Smoothies are a huge part of my healthy cooking repertoire. Whether it's a quick breakfast, a late-night treat, or an afternoon snack to beat an energy slump, a frosty blend of fruits and vegetables—and other ingredients—can be the ultimate refresher.

Even with all the nutritious possibilities, smoothies can be confusing. They have a reputation for being superfoods in a glass, but many of them are sugary milkshakes in disguise. While experts recommend no more than 6 to 9 teaspoons of added sugar a day, most Americans are eating closer to 20! Cutting out 10 teaspoons of sugar per day can lead to a 15-pound weight loss in a year!

What you really want for healthy smoothies are fresh ingredients combined with flavor, color, texture, and nutrition in mind. These recipes are crafted from seasonal, whole food ingredients whirled together to optimize health. Unexpected elements, like green tea powder, dates, chia seeds, and cauliflower (really!), help these blends fully achieve superfood status.

These smoothies are filled with powerful antioxidants to fight inflammation, unsaturated fats for skin and neurological health, minerals for strong bones, and fiber and probiotics to promote gut health—and many contain no added sugar whatsoever.

Each recipe includes a full panel of nutrition information, including a tally of total and added sugars. This is an important distinction to make because natural sugars from dairy and fruit don't wreak havoc on the body the way an abundance of added sugars can.

Within the pages of Healthy, Quick & Easy Smoothies, you'll also find tips, tricks, and mini courses in nutrition to help fuel you every day. Happy blending!

PART 1: SMOOTHIE BASICS

Raise a smoothie glass to your health

Smoothies in this book are packed with nutrient-rich ingredients, don't require fancy equipment, and taste delicious. Plus, they offer three benefits for enjoying a smoothie in today's on-the-go society.

healthy: under 300 calories

No recipe has more than 300 calories—and some have fewer than 100!

quick: 10 minutes to make (or less!)

No recipe takes more than 10 minutes to prep—and most need just 5 minutes.

easy: 5 ingredients (or fewer!)

No recipe has more than 5 ingredients—and several need no more than 2 or 3.

why smoothies are better than juices

This debate between smoothies and juices often focuses on those nutritional differences between the two—as well as, of course, the taste. But it really all comes down to one word: fiber.

Technically, fiber is an indigestible component of plant-based foods. Eating fiber-rich foods helps regulate digestion and increases satiety, making you feel fuller longer. Certain types of fiber can also help lower "bad" cholesterol. Traditional juicing involves extracting liquid from ingredients, like herbs, fruits, and vegetables. While this liquid contains several nutrients, much of the fiber is removed and missing from your glass. The beauty of a smoothie is you get to keep the fiber! While some of the physical composition of the smoothie ingredients are broken down when blended, everything makes its way into your glass—and your body.

choosing and using a blender

Blenders come in many shapes and sizes, and like most kitchen appliances, you get what you pay for. The only way a blender can do you wrong is if the blade easily jams or if the machine is difficult to clean. Shop around and check user reviews when shopping for a product, and be wary of models that fall short in these areas.

All the recipes in this book were made using a Vitamix 5200 Standard blender. This blender is known for its ability to blend everything from frozen fruits to nuts to dry grains. It's certainly worth the high price tag because it lives up to the hype. That said, a pricey blender isn't required to enjoy the recipes in this book.

If you have concerns about your blender's ability to purée with ease, cut harder (or denser) ingredients like nuts, raw beets, carrots, and apples into smaller pieces before adding them to the blender. Also, be sure to add the liquid ingredients first because this always makes for easier blending.

smoothies 101: how to make smoothies

If you can drink it from a glass but it's thick enough to eat with a spoon, then it's a smoothie. And with your blender, you can easily create a smoothie using ingredients from three main categories.

solids

Water content and fiber in an ingredient determine a smoothie's texture and thickness. Bananas have a low water content, but watermelons have a high water content. Pineapple also has a high water content but more fiber than peaches. Smoothies with both get their texture from the pineapple.

liquids

Because portability is critical for smoothies, using various liquids—like 100% fruit juices, coconut and almond milks, freshly squeezed citrus, and coffee and tea—to help purée the ingredients keeps the smoothies thick but drinkable. Water and ice cubes are also often used to help a smoothie stay cold.

binders

Also called emulsifiers, binders help blend ingredients together to form a new mixture and to keep those ingredients from separating. Emulsifiers are often a dairy product (like yogurt) and sometimes a nondairy ingredient (such as nuts). Some fruits can also serve as binders, especially bananas.

serving sizes

Except for the bowls, popsicles, and tubes, all the recipes make two servings, although you can halve or double recipes. You can also freeze unused servings. Make sure to defrost and reblend a frozen smoothie.

making changes

If you decide to make your own modifications, ensure to make swaps with similar ingredients. See Making Modifications & adding Boosters and some of the recipes for specific changes you can make, their benefits, and their impact on calories.

tips for creating better smoothies

Yes, these recipes are quick and easy, but here are some ways to help you make smoothies even more quickly and easily.

save time & money

Prep ingredients ahead of time and store them in resealable plastic bags in the fridge and freezer.
Store overly ripe and slightly mushy bananas and berries in freezer-safe bags for future smoothies.

Buy nuts and seeds in bulk and refrigerate them to increase their shelf life.

If yogurt is nearing its expiration date, pour it into ice cube trays and freeze until needed.

Pour leftover smoothie mixtures into popsicle molds. Kids (and adults!) love these as healthy snacks.

Turn your smoothie into a popsicle!

seasonal suggestions

Eating seasonally is a great way to save money: berries, spinach, and melons in spring and summer and apples, squash, and sweet potatoes in autumn and winter.

Visit your local farmers market for inspiration, and plant an herb garden in your backyard. Because tropical fruits aren't grown in most parts of the country, these are good options to buy frozen.

making modifications & adding boosters

Target specific nutrients to meet your needs. Make swaps or additions to smoothies with these healthy nutrition boosters.

ADDED INGREDIENT	MAIN BENEFIT	ADDITIONAL BENEFITS	ADDED CALORIES
Black tea	Caffeine	Antioxidants, fluoride	1 cup = 2 cals
Brewed coffee	Caffeine	Antioxidants, B vitamins	1 cup = 2 cals
Matcha powder	Caffeine	Antioxidants, neurological function	1 tsp = 7 cals
Coconut water	Electrolytes	Calcium, magnesium	1 cup = 45 cals
Sea salt	Electrolytes	Traces of iron, calcium, zinc, potassium	¼ tsp = 0 cals
Dried prunes	Fiber	Vitamin K	1oz = 65 cals

Wheat germ	Fiber	Iron, selenium	1 tbsp = 50 cals
Chia seeds	Omega-3 fats	Fiber, calcium	1 tbsp = 65 cals
Flaxseed	Omega-3 fats	B vitamins, zinc, magnesium, iron	1 tbsp = 37 cals
Banana flour	Prebiotics	Potassium	2 tbsp = 50 cals
Lentils	Prebiotics	Protein	¼ cup cooked = 55 cals
Low-fat yogurt	Probiotics	Calcium, vitamin D	½ cup = 100 cals
Kefir	Probiotics	Calcium, vitamin D, potassium	½ cup = 55 cals
Kombucha	Probiotics	B vitamins	8oz = 35 cals
Low-fat cottage cheese	Protein	Calcium, vitamin D	½ cup = 80 cals
Nonfat Green yogurt	Protein	Calcium	½ cup = 65 cals
Pea protein powder	Protein	Iron, vegan	2 tbsp = 50 cals
Whey protein powder	Protein	Most absorbable protein	1oz = 120 cals

PART 2: TROPICAL SMOOTHIES

Pineapple & Mango With Orange

Vitamin-rich pineapple and mango are a match made in tropical smoothie heaven, and creamy almond milk adds a dose of calcium and vitamin D.

1 cup unsweetened almond milk

1 cup frozen mango chunks

1 cup frozen pineapple chunks

1 medium orange, juiced

1 In a blender, combine almond milk, mango, pineapple, and orange juice. Blend on high speed until smooth.

2 Pour the mixture into two chilled glasses and serve immediately.

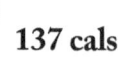

137 cals

2g fat (0g saturated fat), 0mg cholesterol, 92mg sodium, 32g carbohydrates (25g sugar, 0g added sugar, 5g fiber), 2g protein

Pineapple & mango with orange

5 min

4 ingredients

Triple Melon Shake With Mint

This frosty drink is perfect for hot summer days. The trio of melon–watermelon, honeydew, and cantaloupe–provides enough juice that you won't need to add extra liquid.

1½ cups chopped watermelon

1 cup chopped honeydew

1 cup chopped cantaloupe

¼ cup fresh mint leaves

1 In a blender, combine watermelon, honeydew, cantaloupe, mint, and as many ice cubes as needed. Blend on high speed until smooth.

2 Pour the mixture into two chilled glasses and serve immediately.

91 cals

1g fat (0g saturated fat), 0mg cholesterol, 23mg sodium, 16g carbohydrates (13g sugar, 0g added sugar, 2g fiber), 2g protein

10 min

4 ingredients

Banana & Date Shake With Walnuts

With just enough sweetness and even a little bit of crunch, this smoothie will easily become a favorite. And enjoy it even more knowing it doesn't have any added sugar.

2 cups low-fat milk

2 medium bananas

4 dates, pitted and roughly chopped

⅓ cup raw walnut halves

1 In a blender, combine milk, bananas, dates, walnuts, and as many ice cubes as needed. Blend on high speed until well combined, leaving some texture.

2 Pour the mixture into two chilled glasses and serve immediately.

 **300 cals**

9g fat (1g saturated fat), 5mg cholesterol, 105mg sodium, 51g carbohydrates (36g sugar, 0g added sugar, 5g fiber), 12g protein

 **5 min**

 4 ingredients

Watermelon Cooler With Mixed Berries

Sip on this refreshing combo of juicy watermelon and berries. Watermelon is chock-full of lycopene–a powerful antioxidant that fights inflammation and protects against some cancers.

½ cup 100% orange juice

zest and juice of 1 lime, with some zest reserved

2 cups chopped watermelon

1 cup frozen mixed berries

1 In a blender, combine orange juice, lime zest and juice, watermelon, and berries. Blend on high speed until smooth.

2 Pour the mixture into two chilled glasses, top with some lime zest, and serve immediately.

 115 cals

0g fat (0g saturated fat), 0mg cholesterol, 8mg sodium, 28g carbohydrates (19g sugar, 0g added sugar, 4g fiber), 1g protein

 5 min

 4 ingredients

Mango Madness With Banana & Vanilla

If you love mango, then this is your dream smoothie. With its diverse repertoire of vitamins and minerals, mango has rightfully earned superfood status.

1½ cups unsweetened almond milk

2 cups frozen mango

½ medium banana

6oz nonfat mango yogurt

1 tsp pure vanilla extract

1 In a blender, combine almond milk, mango, banana, yogurt, and vanilla extract. Blend on high speed until smooth.

2 Pour the mixture into two chilled glasses and serve immediately.

 **198 cals** 2g fat (0g saturated fat), 3mg cholesterol, 199mg sodium, 42g carbohydrates (32g sugar, 5g added sugar, 4g fiber), 6g protein

 **5 min**

 5 ingredients

Gingersnap Crunch With Bananas & Honey

This smoothie tastes like a dessert but with a minimal amount of added sugar. Plus, ground ginger can help with digestion and blood sugar control.

1½ cups unsweetened soy milk

2 frozen medium bananas

3 graham crackers, crushed

1 tsp ground ginger

1 tbsp honey

1 In a blender, combine soy milk, bananas, graham crackers, ginger, and honey. Blend on high speed until smooth.

2 Pour the mixture into two chilled glasses and serve immediately.

 245 cals

4g fat (1g saturated fat), 0mg cholesterol, 119mg sodium, 48g carbohydrates (27g sugar, 10g added sugar, 4g fiber), 7g protein

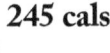 5 min

 5 ingredients

Kiwi & Orange Burst With Strawberries

This is a cool and refreshing drink to enjoy with a meal or as a light snack. Kiwis are filled with vitamin K, which can help keep your blood healthy.

¾ cup 100% orange juice

3 kiwis, peeled and chopped

½ cup frozen strawberries

1 In a blender, combine orange juice, kiwis, and strawberries. Blend on high speed until smooth.

2 Pour the mixture into two chilled glasses and serve immediately.

 **104 cals**   1g fat (0g saturated fat), 0mg cholesterol, 17mg sodium, 25g carbohydrates (17g sugar, 0g added sugar, 3g fiber), 2g protein

 **10 min**

 3 ingredients

Shooting Star Fruit With Peaches & Coconut

This low-calorie, crisp, and refreshing blend of star fruit, peaches, and coconut water gives you a boost of electrolytes. Don't remove the seeds from the star fruit–they're edible!

1 cup coconut water

1 cup frozen peaches

1 large star fruit, sliced

1 Reserve two star fruit slices for garnishing.

2 In a blender, combine coconut water, peaches, and the remaining star fruit. Blend on high speed until smooth.

3 Pour the mixture into two chilled glasses, add a star fruit slice to the side of each glass, and serve immediately.

0g fat (0g saturated fat), 0mg cholesterol, 15mg sodium, 17g carbohydrates (14g sugar, 0g added sugar, 3g fiber), 1g protein

72 cals

5 min

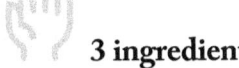

3 ingredients

Goji Berries & Bananas With Coconut

One ounce of goji berries contains almost 150% of your daily vitamin A needs. Their sweet but tart flavor is the perfect complement to toasted coconut and frozen bananas.

⅓ cup unsweetened flaked coconut

1½ cups unsweetened coconut milk

¼ cup dried goji berries

2 medium frozen bananas

1 In a dry pan on the stovetop on medium heat, place coconut flakes and toast until fragrant, about 2 to 3 minutes. Remove the pan from the heat, allow coconut flakes to cool slightly, and reserve 2 tsp for garnishing.

2 In a blender, combine coconut milk, goji berries, bananas, and the remaining toasted coconut. Blend on high speed until smooth.

3 Pour the mixture into two chilled glasses, sprinkle the reserved coconut flakes on top, and serve immediately.

 **287 cals**

12g fat (11g saturated fat), 0mg cholesterol, 107mg sodium, 31g carbohydrates (22g sugar, 0g added sugar, 6g fiber), 3g protein

 10 min

 4 ingredients

Dragon Fruit Dream With Raspberries & Honey

Dragon fruit is a tropical fruit that contains carbs, iron, magnesium, and hunger-fighting fiber. You can find fresh dragon fruit in autumn and winter or frozen year-round.

1½ cups unsweetened coconut milk beverage

1 cup frozen dragon fruit

¼ cup freeze-dried raspberries

1 tbsp honey

juice of ½ lime

1 In a blender, combine coconut milk, dragon fruit, and raspberries. Blend on high speed until smooth.

2 Add honey and lime juice, and blend on high speed again until smooth.

3 Pour the mixture into two chilled glasses and serve immediately.

 **147 cals**

3g fat (3g saturated fat), 0mg cholesterol, 28mg sodium, 27g carbohydrates (27g sugar, 8g added sugar, 5g fiber), 2g protein

 5 min

 5 ingredients

Pom Pom With Clementine

Once just an obscure fruit, pomegranates are now almost everywhere. Because the arils–the seed pods–also have antioxidants, this smoothie features the pods and the juice.

1 clementine, zested and peeled

2 cups pomegranate juice

1 cup low-fat Greek yogurt

¼ cup pomegranate arils

1 In a blender, combine clementine zest and flesh, pomegranate juice, yogurt, pomegranate arils, and as many ice cubes as needed. Blend on high speed until smooth.

2 Pour the mixture into two chilled glasses and serve immediately.

 **215 cals**

3g fat (2g saturated fat), 8mg cholesterol, 50mg sodium, 39g carbohydrates (33g sugar, 0g added sugar, 1g fiber), 10g protein

 **5 min**

 4 ingredients

Pineapple Mojito With Lime & Mint

This contains vitamin C and bromelain from the pineapple to fight inflammation throughout the body. Kombucha adds probiotics to support a healthy digestive system.

juice of 2 limes

1¼ cups pineapple kombucha

1 cup frozen pineapple

5 mint leaves

1 In a blender, combine lime juice, kombucha, pineapple, and mint. Blend on high speed until smooth.

2 Pour the mixture into two chilled glasses and serve immediately.

63 cals

0g fat (0g saturated fat), 0mg cholesterol, 14mg sodium, 16g carbohydrates (12g sugar, 3g added sugar, 0g fiber), 1g protein

5 min

4 ingredients

Guava & Mango Lassi With Chia Seeds & Coconut

Nothing tastes quite like guava, and it offers a healthy dose of vitamin C. Because fresh guava can be hard to find, choose a guava nectar with minimal added sugar.

8oz guava nectar

½ cup low-fat milk

1 cup frozen mango

1 tsp chia seeds

1 tsp shredded coconut

1 In a blender, combine ¼ cup water, guava nectar, milk, and mango. Blend on high speed until smooth.

2 Pour the mixture into two chilled glasses, sprinkle chia seeds and shredded coconut on top, and serve immediately.

 **162 cals**

 **5 min**

 5 ingredients

2g fat (1g saturated fat), 3mg cholesterol, 37mg sodium, 37g carbohydrates (31g sugar, 8g added sugar, 3g fiber), 3g protein

Pineapple & Coconut With Banana & Honey

This smoothie is tropical goodness. Frozen pineapple is a healthy game-changer, adding texture and antioxidants, like bromelain, which is a potent inflammation fighter.

1¾ cups unsweetened coconut milk beverage

1½ cups frozen pineapple

1 medium banana

2 tsp honey

2 tbsp unsweetened dried coconut flakes

1 In a blender, combine coconut milk, pineapple, banana, honey, and coconut flakes. Blend on high speed until smooth.

2 Pour the mixture into two chilled glasses and serve immediately.

 **213 cals**

9g fat (5g saturated fat), 0mg cholesterol, 84mg sodium, 35g carbohydrates (24g sugar, 5g added sugar, 4g fiber), 2g protein

 **5 min**

 5 ingredients

Banana & Mango Pops With Coconut & Honey

Although this smoothie is packed with nutritional goodness, it has just 30 calories per serving. You could add cinnamon for a sharp tang or use cayenne pepper for an extra kick.

¾ cup unsweetened coconut milk beverage

1 cup frozen mango

½ medium banana

1 tbsp honey

1 In a blender, combine coconut milk, mango, banana, and honey. Blend on high speed until smooth.

2 Pour the mixture into eight popsicle molds and freeze for at least 6 hours or overnight before serving.

1g fat (0g saturated fat), 0mg cholesterol, 4mg sodium, 7g carbohydrates (5g sugar, 0g added sugar, 1g fiber), 0g protein

30 cals

5 min

4 ingredients

Blood Orange Margarita With Peaches & Key Lime

Blood oranges and key lime yogurt create a zing of flavor and offer vitamin C. This nonalcoholic tribute to the famous cocktail also offers 8 grams of fiber per serving.

2 blood oranges, peeled

5oz low-fat key lime Greek yogurt

1½ cups frozen peaches

1 cup seltzer

1 In a blender, combine oranges, yogurt, peaches, and seltzer. Blend on high speed until smooth.

2 Pour the mixture into two chilled glasses and serve immediately.

 **169 cals** 1g fat (1g saturated fat), 8mg cholesterol, 57mg sodium, 35g carbohydrates (29g sugar, 8g added sugar, 5g fiber), 8g protein

 5 min

 4 ingredients

Açaí & Pineapple Bowl With Chia Seeds & Walnuts

Enjoy this thick, spoonable blend of tropical superfoods topped with crunchy nuts and seeds (more superfoods!). This version uses freezer packs of unsweetened açaí purée.

½ pack frozen açaí purée

1 cup frozen pineapple

⅓ cup soy milk

1 tbsp chia seeds

2 tbsp chopped walnuts

1 Place açaí purée packet in a small bowl, cover with warm water, and let sit for 1 minute. This helps with blending the açaí.

2 In a blender, combine thawed açaí purée, pineapple, and soy milk. Blend on high speed for 20 seconds, stop the blender, and stir. Repeat until smooth.

3 Pour the mixture into a medium bowl, sprinkle chia seeds and walnuts on top, and serve immediately.

 **275 cals**   13g fat (2g saturated fat), 0mg cholesterol, 52mg sodium, 37g carbohydrates (19g sugar, 0g added sugar, 10g fiber), 7g protein

 **10 min**

 5 ingredients

Coconut Quartet With Lime

You'll find not one, not two, not three, but four ways to love coconut in this tropical blend. You'll also enjoy a hint of lime in this take on a stripped-down nonalcoholic coconut mojito.

1 cup coconut water

1 cup unsweetened coconut milk beverage

¾ cup coconut Greek yogurt

2 tbsp dried unsweetened coconut

juice of ½ lime

1 To make the ice cubes, pour coconut water into an ice cube tray and freeze until solid.

2 In a blender, combine coconut milk, coconut water ice cubes, yogurt, and dried coconut. Add more water ice cubes as needed. Blend on high speed until smooth.

3 Pour the mixture into two chilled glasses and serve immediately.

 **205 cals** 13g fat (12g saturated fat), 8mg cholesterol, 77mg sodium, 16g carbohydrates (12g sugar, 4g added sugar, 3g fiber), 7g protein

 5 min

 4 ingredients

Grapefruit Detox With Green Tea & Beet

Forget those fad juices. Why not drink something that can actually help cleanse your system? This tea offers plenty of purifying antioxidants–and it's refreshing!

¾ cup chilled brewed green tea

juice of 1 large grapefruit

1 tbsp beet juice

1 In a blender, combine green tea, grapefruit juice, beet juice, and as many ice cubes as needed. Blend on high speed until completely mixed.

2 Pour the mixture into two chilled glasses and serve immediately.

 **58 cals** 0g fat (0g saturated fat), 0mg cholesterol, 0mg sodium, 15g carbohydrates (12g sugar, 0g added sugar, 2g fiber), 1g protein

 **5 min**

 3 ingredients

Lychee & Lemon With Coconut

The sweet and floral scent of lychee makes for a glorious summer fruit. Because they're often packed in sugar syrup, drain the syrup before adding the lychee to the blender.

1½ cups unsweetened coconut milk beverage

½ cup canned lychee, drained

juice of ½ lemon

1 In a blender, combine coconut milk, lychee, lemon juice, and as many ice cubes as needed. Blend on high speed until smooth.

2 Pour the mixture into two chilled glasses and serve immediately.

3g fat (3g saturated fat), 0mg cholesterol, 26mg sodium, 15g carbohydrates (15g sugar, 5g added sugar, 1g fiber), 1g protein

 **97 cals**

 **5 min**

 3 ingredients

Roasted Pineapple With Cottage Cheese

This smoothie has just three ingredients, but it's the complete package. Every sip offers protein, healthy carbs, electrolytes, and fluids–great after a workout for optimal recovery.

2 cups fresh pineapple

1½ cups coconut water

½ cup low-fat cottage cheese

1 Preheat your oven to broil. Place pineapple in a broiler-safe pan and broil until bubbly, about 5 minutes. Remove pineapple from the pan and set aside to cool for 2 to 3 minutes.

2 In a blender, combine cooled broiled pineapple, coconut water, cottage cheese, and as many ice cubes as needed. Blend on high speed until smooth.

3 Pour the mixture into two chilled glasses and serve immediately.

1g fat (1g saturated fat), 15mg cholesterol, 352mg sodium, 58g carbohydrates (43g sugar, 0g added sugar, 0g fiber), 16g protein

286 cals

10 min

3 ingredients

Pineapple & Spinach With Cilantro & Ginger

This frosty blend of pineapple, spinach, and cilantro will taste light and refreshing. Fresh ginger seals the deal on this must-have drink that's filled with herbaceous goodness.

1½ cups low-fat milk

1 cup frozen pineapple

½ cup chopped spinach

¼ cup chopped cilantro

½ tsp freshly grated ginger

1 In a blender, combine milk, pineapple, spinach, cilantro, ginger, and black pepper to taste. Blend on high speed until smooth.

2 Pour the mixture into two chilled glasses and serve immediately.

2g fat (1g saturated fat), 8mg cholesterol, 85mg sodium, 21g carbohydrates (17g sugar, 0g added sugar, 1g fiber), 7g protein

126 cals

5 min

5 ingredients

Açaí & Peach Bowl With Pineapple & Orange

This spoonable smoothie packs 14 grams of tummy-pleasing fiber into each serving. Add a scoop of pea protein powder for a high-protein vegan breakfast.

1 pack frozen açaí purée

1 cup frozen peaches

zest and juice of 1 orange

2 tbsp chopped pineapple

1 tbsp unsweetened shredded coconut

1 Place açaí purée packet in a small bowl, cover with warm water, and let sit for 1 minute. This helps with blending the açaí.

2 In a blender, combine ¼ cup water, thawed açaí purée, peaches, orange zest and juice. Blend on high speed for 30 seconds, stop the blender, and stir. Repeat until smooth.

3 Pour the mixture into a medium bowl, sprinkle pineapple and shredded coconut on top, and serve immediately.

 **267 cals**

9g fat (4g saturated fat), 0mg cholesterol, 25mg sodium, 48g carbohydrates (14g sugar, 0g added sugar, 14g fiber), 4g protein

 **10 min**

 **5 ingredients**

Passion Fruit With Orange & Banana

Passion fruit adds a one-of-a-kind flavor to smoothies, and it's also high in antioxidants. And add the seeds because they'll provide a bit of pleasant crunch to each sip.

¾ cup 100% orange juice

3 small passion fruit, halved and flesh scooped out

1 frozen medium banana

1 In a blender, combine ¼ cup water, orange juice, passion fruit, and banana. Blend on high speed until smooth.

2 Pour the mixture into two chilled glasses and serve immediately.

 **116 cals**

0g fat (0g saturated fat), 0mg cholesterol, 23mg sodium, 28g carbohydrates (17g sugar, 0g added sugar, 4g fiber), 2g protein

 **5 min**

 3 ingredients

Papaya & Honey With Flaxseed

Inflammation-fighting properties from papaya and flaxseed make this smoothie a top choice when you're fighting a cold. Peel, chop, and freeze fresh papaya for up to 6 months.

1 cup unsweetened coconut milk beverage

½ fresh papaya, seeds removed and flesh scooped out

2 tbsp honey

2 tbsp ground flaxseed

1 In a blender, combine coconut milk, papaya, honey, flaxseed, and as many ice cubes as needed. Blend on high speed until smooth.

2 Pour the mixture into two chilled glasses and serve immediately.

157 cals

5g fat (2g saturated fat), 0mg cholesterol, 24mg sodium, 28g carbohydrates (23g sugar, 17g added sugar, 3g fiber), 2g protein

5 min

4 ingredients

PART 3: BERRY SMOOTHIES

Wild Blueberry Blast With Banana & Chia Seeds

This contains protein, carbs, electrolytes, and antioxidants. In fact, wild blueberries have more antioxidants than regular blueberries, and freezing them actually boosts their power.

½ cup 100% orange juice

1 medium banana

1½ cups frozen wild blueberries

1 cup low-fat cottage cheese

1 tbsp chia seeds

1 In a blender, combine ½ cup water, orange juice, banana, wild blueberries, cottage cheese, and chia seeds. Blend on high speed until smooth.

2 Pour the mixture into two chilled glasses and serve immediately.

2g fat (1g saturated fat), 15mg cholesterol, 350mg sodium, 41g carbohydrates (16g sugar, 0g added sugar, 8g fiber), 16g protein

 **246 cals**

 **5 min**

 5 ingredients

Oats & Strawberries With Blueberries

Fiber-rich rolled oats can turn a smoothie into a meal. In fact, the soluble fiber in oats and berries can support heart health by helping lower "bad" cholesterol.

1½ cups vanilla almond milk

½ cup frozen strawberries

½ cup frozen blueberries

½ cup rolled oats

1 In a blender, combine almond milk, strawberries, blueberries, and oats. Blend on high speed until smooth.

2 Pour the mixture into two chilled glasses and serve immediately.

 **134 cals** 4g fat (0g saturated fat), 0mg cholesterol, 94mg sodium, 23g carbohydrates (6g sugar, 0g added sugar, 4g fiber), 4g protein

 **5 min**

 4 ingredients

Blackberries & Banana With Coconut

Ready to enjoy the ideal balance of sweet, tart, and creamy? This fruit-heavy smoothie has health doses of potassium, fiber, and calcium but only 126 calories per serving.

1½ cups unsweetened coconut milk beverage

1 cup fresh or frozen blackberries

1 medium frozen banana

1 In a blender, combine coconut milk, blackberries, and banana. Blend on high speed until smooth.

2 Pour the mixture into two chilled glasses and serve immediately.

 **126 cals**

4g fat (3g saturated fat), 0mg cholesterol, 27mg sodium, 24g carbohydrates (15g sugar, 0g added sugar, 5g fiber), 1g protein

 **5 min**

 3 ingredients

Chocolate & Cherries With a Pinch Of Sea Salt

Because chocolate milk and fresh cherries contain nutrients that muscles need after exercise, why not team them up? Adding a little sea salt enhances their flavors.

1½ cups low-fat chocolate milk

2 cups frozen sweet cherries

1 In a blender, combine chocolate milk, cherries, and a pinch of sea salt (if using). Blend on high speed until smooth.

2 Pour the mixture into two chilled glasses and serve immediately.

 **230 cals**

 **5 min**

 2 ingredients

2g fat (1g saturated fat), 6mg cholesterol, 181mg sodium, 48g carbohydrates (38g sugar, 18g added sugar, 4g fiber), 8g protein

Raspberry Creamsicles With Banana & Honey

Cool off with these marvously berry-rific ice pops. They have less sugar than anything you'd find in the freezer sections—and they're more nutritious and delicious!

¾ cup low-fat milk

1 cup fresh raspberries

1 medium banana

1 tbsp honey

1 In a blender, combine milk, raspberries, banana, and honey. Blend on high speed until smooth.

2 Pour the mixture into eight popsicle molds and freeze for at least 6 hours or overnight before serving.

0g fat (0g saturated fat), 1mg cholesterol, 13mg sodium, 9g carbohydrates (6g sugar, 2g added sugar, 1g fiber), 1g protein

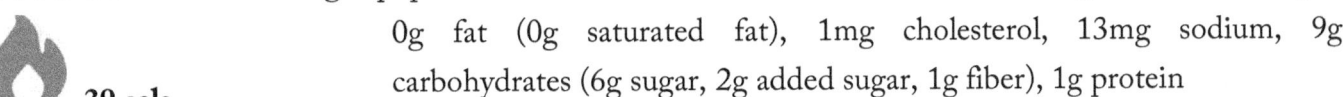 39 cals

 5 min

 4 ingredients

Nectarine Tubes With Blackberries

Disposable smoothie tubes turn sippable delights into handheld treats. They're also a wonderful way to recycle smoothie leftovers into easy-to-hold frozen treats.

¾ cup unsweetened canned coconut milk

1 nectarine, pitted and chopped

1 cup blackberries

1 tbsp honey

1 In a blender, combine coconut milk, nectarine, blackberries, and honey. Blend on high speed until smooth.

2 Pour the mixture into four tube molds and seal closed. Lay flat in the freezer until frozen, about 4 hours, before serving.

 **135 cals**

8g fat (5g saturated fat), 0mg cholesterol, 24mg sodium, 15g carbohydrates (11g sugar, 4g added sugar, 3g fiber), 2g protein

 **5 min**

 4 ingredients

Raspberry Brûlée With Cream Cheese

Adding a little heat to fresh raspberries releases the natural sugars and brings out their flavor. This smoothie will remind you of a (much healthier) version of a crème brûlée.

½ pint fresh raspberries

1 tbsp light brown sugar

1½ cups low-fat milk

1 tbsp light cream cheese

1 Preheat your oven to broil. Place raspberries in a broiler-safe pan, sprinkle with brown sugar, and broil until sugar is melted and raspberries are slightly charred, about 2 to 3 minutes. Remove the pan from the oven and set aside for 2 to 3 minutes to allow raspberries to cool.

2 In a blender, combine carmelized raspberries, milk, cream cheese, and as many ice cubes as needed. Blend on high speed until smooth.

3 Pour the mixture into two chilled glasses and serve immediately.

152 cals

3g fat (2g saturated fat), 11mg cholesterol, 136mg sodium, 24g carbohydrates (18g sugar, 6g added sugar, 4g fiber), 7g protein

10 min

4 ingredients

Red Currants & Honey With Banana & Coconut

Red currants are berries similar to cranberries but juicier. They're underappreciated berries but feature ellagic acid– a compound that has some cancer-fighting properties.

1½ cups coconut water

1 cup red currants

2 tbsp wildflower honey

1 frozen medium banana

1 In a blender, combine coconut water, red currants, honey, and banana. Blend on high speed until smooth.

2 Pour the mixture into two chilled glasses and serve immediately.

 **177 cals**

0g fat (0g saturated fat), 0mg cholesterol, 46mg sodium, 47g carbohydrates (35g sugar, 17g added sugar, 4g fiber), 1g protein

 **5 min**

 4 ingredients

Blueberry Cheesecake With Banana & Vanilla

If you're craving cheesecake, try this high-protein smoothie instead. Because banana adds natural sweetness, there's no added sugar—and thus no added calories.

2 cups unsweetened almond milk

2 cups frozen blueberries

1 cup nonfat cottage cheese

1 medium banana

1 tsp pure vanilla extract

1 In a blender, combine almond milk, blueberries, cottage cheese, banana, and vanilla extract. Blend on high speed until smooth.

2 Pour the mixture into two chilled glasses and serve immediately.

254 cals

3g fat (0g saturated fat), 5mg cholesterol, 430mg sodium, 37g carbohydrates (26g sugar, 0g added sugar, 7g fiber), 18g protein

5 min

5 ingredients

Mixed Berry Crunch With a Touch Of Honey

Granola adds a satisfying crunch to this antioxidant-rich smoothie that's bursting with mixed berries and sweetened by honey. Add a little water if this smoothie seems too thick.

2 cups unsweetened soy milk

2 cups frozen mixed berries

1 tbsp honey

4 tbsp granola, divided

1 In a blender, combine soy milk, berries, and honey. Blend on high speed until smooth.

2 Add 3 tbsp granola and blend again on high speed until combined, leaving some texture.

3 Pour the mixture into two chilled glasses, sprinkle the remaining 1 tbsp granola on top, and serve immediately.

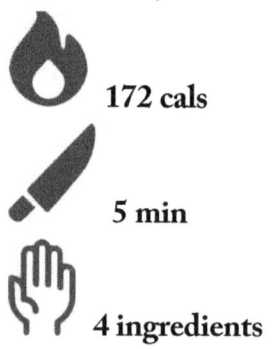

172 cals

5 min

4 ingredients

3g fat (0g saturated fat), 0mg cholesterol, 72mg sodium, 34g carbohydrates (20g sugar, 9g added sugar, 5g fiber), 5g protein

Raspberries & Chia Seeds With a Hint Of Maple

With a whopping 11 grams of fiber and 15 grams of protein, this sweet purple smoothie will satisfy for hours after that first sip. And chia seeds offer a little crunch.

1½ cups skim milk

3oz nonfat raspberry Greek yogurt

2 cups frozen raspberries

2 tsp 100% maple syrup

1 tbsp chia seeds

1 In a blender, combine milk, yogurt, raspberries, maple syrup, and chia seeds. Blend on high speed until smooth.

2 Pour the mixture into two chilled glasses and serve immediately.

 **226 cals**

3g fat (0g saturated fat), 4mg cholesterol, 108mg sodium, 38g carbohydrates (25g sugar, 10g added sugar, 11g fiber), 15g protein

 **5 min**

 5 ingredients

Strawberry Delight With Rhubarb & Honey

This seasonal treasure has a tangy flare that's the perfect complement to sun-sweet strawberries. This smoothie is also an excellent source of vitamin C.

1 small stalk rhubarb, finely chopped

1 tbsp honey

2 cups frozen strawberries

½ cup low-fat strawberry yogurt

1 Place rhubarb and honey in a microwave-safe bowl. Cook on high for 2 minutes. Set aside to cool for 2 to 3 minutes.

2 In a blender, combine 1 cup water, cooled rhubarb, strawberries, and yogurt. Blend on high speed until smooth, adding more water a little at a time as needed.

3 Pour the mixture into two chilled glasses and serve immediately.

144 cals

2g fat (1g saturated fat), 3mg cholesterol, 44mg sodium, 33g carbohydrates (27g sugar, 12g added sugar, 3g fiber), 3g protein

10 min

4 ingredients

Strawberries & Vanilla With Lavender

A member of the mint family, lavender is worth eating more often. It's sweet and floral, and it can calm and soothe. Plus, it's a lovely complement to strawberries.

2 cups unsweetened soy milk

2 cups frozen strawberries

1 tbsp honey

1 tbsp chopped dried lavender leaves

2 tsp pure vanilla extract

1 In a blender, combine soy milk, strawberries, honey, lavender leaves, and vanilla extract. Blend on high speed until smooth.

2 Pour the mixture into two chilled glasses and serve immediately.

 **175 cals**   5g fat (1g saturated fat), 0mg cholesterol, 96mg sodium, 27g carbohydrates (19g sugar, 8g added sugar, 3g fiber), 8g protein

 **5 min**

 5 ingredients

Roasted Grapes With Banana

Grapes are botanically berries, and roasting them brings their sweetness to another level. Use a combination of red and green grapes for an even more unexpected smoothie experience.

2 cups halved grapes

1 frozen medium banana

1 Preheat the oven to 425°F (218°C). Place grapes on a baking pan and roast for 7 minutes. Remove the pan from the oven, transfer grapes to a small bowl, and place the bowl in the freezer for 3 to 4 minutes.

2 In a blender, combine 1 cup water, cooled grapes, and banana. Blend on high speed until smooth.

3 Pour the mixture into two chilled glasses and serve immediately.

 **228 cals**

1g fat (0g saturated fat), 0mg cholesterol, 14mg sodium, 59g carbohydrates (44g sugar, 0g added sugar, 5g fiber), 2g protein

 10 min

 2 ingredients

Strawberry Sundae With Banana

This classic smoothie is all about the basics. This version is made with frozen fruit, skim milk, and Greek yogurt for extra protein. Leftovers make great popsicles.

1 cup skim milk

1 large frozen banana

1 cup frozen strawberries

½ cup nonfat strawberry Greek yogurt

1 In a blender, combine ½ cup water, milk, banana, strawberries, and yogurt. Blend on high speed until smooth.

2 Pour the mixture into two chilled glasses and serve immediately.

 **168 cals**

0g fat (0g saturated fat), 6mg cholesterol, 86mg sodium, 35g carbohydrates (23g sugar, 7g added sugar, 3g fiber), 10g protein

 **5 min**

 4 ingredients

Fruit Salad Surprise With Coconut & Chia Seeds

Transfer leftover fruit salad to freezer-safe bags. Use it for this recipe to reduce food waste and to sip on a delicious blend of flavors that's a little different every time.

1 cup coconut water

2 cups frozen fruit salad

1 tbsp chia seeds

2 tsp unsweetened shredded coconut

1 In a blender, combine coconut water and fruit salad. Blend on high speed until smooth.

2 Pour the mixture into two chilled glasses, sprinkle chia seeds and shredded coconut on top, and serve immediately.

 **222 cals**

 **5 min**

 4 ingredients

4g fat (2g saturated fat), 0mg cholesterol, 65mg sodium, 46g carbohydrates (26g sugar, 0g added sugar, 10g fiber), 3g protein

Pb & J Shake With Banana & Oats

Imagine a peanut butter sandwich and a cold glass of milk whirled into a smoothie. This sippable treat has no added sugar and makes a fabulous breakfast or snack.

1¾ cups nonfat milk

2 tbsp natural peanut butter

⅓ cup rolled oats

1 medium frozen banana

1 cup frozen strawberries

1 In a blender, combine milk, peanut butter, oats, banana, and strawberries. Blend on high speed until smooth.

2 Pour the mixture into two chilled glasses and serve immediately.

 **300 cals**

10g fat (2g saturated fat), 4mg cholesterol, 98mg sodium, 43g carbohydrates (20g sugar, 0g added sugar, 5g fiber), 15g protein

 5 min

 5 ingredients

Three-Layer Berry Treat With Apple & Honey

Berries have amazing antioxidant power! And the trick to this smoothie is to make the layers thick enough so they don't all mix together until you're ready to slurp it down.

½ cup 100% apple juice

1 cup frozen wild blueberries

1 cup frozen mixed berries, divided

1¼ cups unsweetened soy milk, divided

3 tsp honey, divided

1 In a blender, combine apple juice and blueberries. Blend on high speed until smooth. Pour the mixture into two glasses and place them in the fridge.

2 In a clean blender, combine ¾ cup mixed berries, ½ cup soy milk, and 1 tsp honey. Blend on high speed until smooth. Add a little water if the mixture becomes too thick. Pour the mixture on top of the blueberries layer and place the glasses in the fridge.

3 In a clean blender, combine the remaining ¼ cup berries, ¾ cup soy milk, and 2 tsp honey. Blend on high speed until smooth. Pour the mixture on top of the mixed berries layer and serve immediately.

4g fat (0g saturated fat), 0mg cholesterol, 87mg sodium, 36g carbohydrates (20g sugar, 8g added sugar, 6g fiber), 7g protein

200 cals

10 min

5 ingredients

Cranberry Rejuvenator With Orange

Frozen cranberries add a tart edge to smoothies. Research links them to many health benefits, including lower blood pressure, reduced cancer risk, and resolving urinary tract infections.

1 cup orange juice, preferably freshly squeezed

1 cup frozen cranberries

¾ cup vanilla Greek yogurt

1 In a blender, combine orange juice, cranberries, and yogurt. Blend on high speed until smooth.

2 Pour the mixture into two chilled glasses and serve immediately.

135 cals

0g fat (0g saturated fat), 0mg cholesterol, 52mg sodium, 24g carbohydrates (17g sugar, 4g added sugar, 2g fiber), 10g protein

5 min

3 ingredients

Mixed Berries & Beet With Banana & Lemon

Ever try drinking your beets? This root veggie is filled with compounds that can help benefit liver health, promote circulation, and lower blood pressure.

1 cup beet juice

1 cup frozen mixed berries

1 frozen medium banana

zest and juice of 1 lemon

1 In a blender, combine ½ cup water, beet juice, mixed berries, banana, and lemon zest and juice. Blend on high speed until smooth.

2 Pour the mixture into two chilled glasses and serve immediately.

 **146 cals**

0g fat (0g saturated fat), 0mg cholesterol, 38mg sodium, 36g carbohydrates (25g sugar, 0g added sugar, 4g fiber), 2g protein

 5 min

 4 ingredients

Strawberries & Pineapple With Orange

This recipe will quickly become your kids' (and maybe your) all-time favorite smoothie—and it's easy to see why because it's bursting with flavor, colors, and vitamins!

zest and juice of 1 orange

1 cup frozen pineapple

1 cup frozen strawberries

¾ cup low-fat strawberry yogurt

1 In a blender, combine 1½ cups water, orange zest and juice, pineapple, strawberries, and yogurt. Blend on high speed until smooth.

2 Pour the mixture into two chilled glasses and serve immediately.

 188 cals

2g fat (0g saturated fat), 6mg cholesterol, 61mg sodium, 41g carbohydrates (23g sugar, 5g added sugar, 6g fiber), 6g protein

 5 min

 4 ingredients

Mixed Berry Shock With Beet

Tart flavors from citrus yogurt and berries balance out the earthiness of fresh beets. And beets are great for promoting heart and liver health.

1 cup lime seltzer

¾ cup lime Greek yogurt

1 medium beet, peeled and chopped

1 cup frozen mixed berries

1 In a blender, combine seltzer, yogurt, beet, and berries. Blend on high speed until smooth.

2 Pour the mixture into two chilled glasses and serve immediately.

 **113 cals**

0g fat (0g saturated fat), 0mg cholesterol, 101mg sodium, 18g carbohydrates (14g sugar, 4g added sugar, 4g fiber), 10g protein

 **5 min**

 4 ingredients

Tart Cherry Shake With Vanilla

Cherry juice can help fight inflammation in tired muscles, and this smoothie gives the body exactly what it needs. For best results, drink within 60 minutes after exercise.

1 cup tart cherry juice

2 cups frozen pitted cherries

4 tbsp vanilla protein powder

1 In a blender, combine 1 cup water, cherry juice, cherries, and vanilla protein powder. Blend on high speed until smooth.

2 Pour the mixture into two chilled glasses and serve immediately.

 **267 cals**

2g fat (1g saturated fat), 8mg cholesterol, 114mg sodium, 49g carbohydrates (32g sugar, 4g added sugar, 4g fiber), 17g protein

 **5 min**

 3 ingredients

Strawberries & Hemp With a Hint Of Maple

Nutrient-dense hemp seeds are an amazing superfood. With a subtle nutty flavor and an impressive amount of healthy fats, they're perfect for a healthy smoothie.

2 cups hemp milk

2 cups frozen strawberries

zest and juice of 1 lime

2 tbsp hemp seeds, divided

2 tsp maple syrup

1 In a blender, combine hemp milk, lime zest and juice, strawberries, 1 tbsp hemp seeds, and maple syrup. Blend on high speed until smooth.

2 Pour the mixture into two chilled glasses, sprinkle the remaining 1 tbsp hemp seeds on top, and serve immediately.

 **191 cals**

10g fat (0g saturated fat), 0mg cholesterol, 116mg sodium, 23g carbohydrates (15g sugar, 5g added sugar, 4g fiber), 8g protein

 **5 min**

 5 ingredients

Backyard Berries With Vanilla Frozen Yogurt

Nothing's more delectable than a freshly picked berry because that's when its nutrient content is at its absolute peak. Visit your local farmers market to buy berries that are in season.

1 cup skim milk

½ cup strawberries

½ cup blueberries

½ cup raspberries

¾ cup nonfat vanilla frozen yogurt

1 In a blender, combine milk, strawberries, blueberries, raspberries, and frozen yogurt. Blend on high speed until smooth.

2 Pour the mixture into two chilled glasses and serve immediately.

166 cals

5 min

5 ingredients

1g fat (0g saturated fat), 5mg cholesterol, 106mg sodium, 34g carbohydrates (28g sugar, 9g added sugar, 3g fiber), 8g protein

PART 4: COMBO SMOOTHIES

Carrots & Apples With a Splash Of Lemon

This smoothie offers a huge boost of vitamin A to promote healthy skin. Leave the skin on the apples for more fiber, and serve this refreshing juice blend poured over ice.

2 cups chopped carrots

2 small apples, Gala or Fuji varieties recommended cored and chopped

juice of 1 lemon

1 In a blender, combine 2 cups water, carrots, apples, and lemon juice. Blend on high speed until smooth.

2 Pour the mixture into two chilled glasses—over ice if desired—and serve immediately.

0g fat (0g saturated fat), 0mg cholesterol, 69mg sodium, 31g carbohydrates (20g sugar, 0g added sugar, 7g fiber), 1g protein

133 cals

5 min

3 ingredients

Pumpkin Pie With Maple & Flaxseed

A squash like pumpkin has plenty of vitamin A, riboflavin, and hunger-fighting fiber. Make sure to buy unsweetened canned pumpkin, not sugary pumpkin pie filling.

1½ cups unsweetened almond milk

2 tbsp maple syrup

1 cup canned pumpkin purée

3 tbsp ground flaxseed

1 In a blender, combine almond milk, maple syrup, pumpkin purée, flaxseed, and as many ice cubes as needed. Blend on high speed until smooth.

2 Pour the mixture into two chilled glasses and serve immediately.

 **164 cals**

6g fat (0g saturated fat), 0mg cholesterol, 120mg sodium, 26g carbohydrates (18g sugar, 13g added sugar, 9g fiber), 5g protein

 5 min

 4 ingredients

Chocolate Shake With Cauliflower

You won't taste the cauliflower, but you'll take advantage of its cancer-fighting properties. Make this after a workout or without the protein powder for a mid-day snack.

1 cup low-fat chocolate milk

1 cup nonfat milk

1 frozen medium banana

1 cup frozen cauliflower florets

4 tbsp chocolate protein powder

1 In a blender, combine chocolate milk, nonfat milk, banana, cauliflower, and protein powder. Blend on high speed until smooth.

2 Pour the mixture into two chilled glasses and serve immediately.

 **232 cals**

2g fat (1g saturated fat), 10mg cholesterol, 237mg sodium, 36g carbohydrates (27g sugar, 8g added sugar, 3g fiber), 20g protein

 **5 min**

 5 ingredients

Golden Butternut With a Touch Of Honey

The natural sweetness and creamy texture of nutrient-rich butternut squash is perfect for this delicious smoothie. It's also surprisingly high in protein.

1½ cups vanilla almond milk

2 cups chopped frozen butternut squash

1 tbsp honey

1 In a blender, combine almond milk, butternut, and honey. Blend on high speed until smooth.

2 Pour the mixture into two chilled glasses and serve immediately.

281 cals

4g fat (0g saturated fat), 0mg cholesterol, 95mg sodium, 61g carbohydrates (17g sugar, 8g added sugar, 2g fiber), 7g protein

5 min

3 ingredients

Pineapple & Chia Bowl With Banana & Orange

This is a fun blend of succulent flavors with a hint of citrus. You'll also get a healthy dose of omega-3 fats from the chia seeds. Zest the oranges before using and sprinkle on top.

1¼ cups unsweetened almond milk

2 cups frozen pineapple

1 medium banana, sliced, divided

1 tbsp chia seeds

2 medium oranges

1 In a blender, combine almond milk, pineapple, ½ banana, and 2 tsp chia seeds. Cut oranges in half and squeeze the juice into the blender. Blend on high speed until smooth.

2 Pour the mixture into two medium bowls, sprinkle chia seeds and the remaining banana slices on top, and serve immediately.

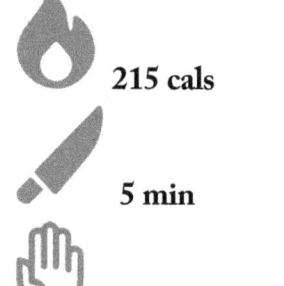

215 cals

5 min

5 ingredients

5g fat (0g saturated fat), 0mg cholesterol, 115mg sodium, 46g carbohydrates (30g sugar, 0g added sugar, 9g fiber), 4g protein

Tomatoes & Basil With a Splash Of Lemon

This is a glass of pure refreshment that features the antioxidant lycopene–a plant-based substance that might help protect against heart disease and certain types of cancer.

2 plum tomatoes, stems removed

2 tbsp chopped basil

1 tbsp freshly squeezed lemon juice

1 In a blender, combine 1 cup water, tomatoes, basil, lemon, and a pinch of kosher salt. Blend on high speed until smooth,

2 Pour the mixture into two chilled glasses and serve immediately.

 13 cals

0g fat (0g saturated fat), 0mg cholesterol, 79mg sodium, 3g carbohydrates (2g sugar, 0g added sugar, 1g fiber), 1g protein

 5 min

 3 ingredients

Peanut Butter Shake With Cottage Cheese

Powdered peanut butter has 85% less calories and fat than regular peanut butter, making it perfect for smoothies. In this blend, cottage cheese packs in the protein.

1¾ cups skim milk

2 frozen medium bananas

¼ cup powdered peanut butter

¾ cup low-fat cottage cheese

1 In a blender, combine milk, banana, powdered peanut butter, and cottage cheese. Blend on high speed until smooth.

2 Pour the mixture into two chilled glasses and serve immediately.

 257 cals   1g fat (0g saturated fat), 6mg cholesterol, 278mg sodium, 42g carbohydrates (26g sugar, 0g added sugar, 4g fiber), 23g protein

 5 min

 4 ingredients

Pumpkin Power With Banana & Maple

There's no actual pumpkin in this, but the pumpkin protein powder has a tremendous amount of vegan protein! Instead of maple syrup, use dried dates to sweeten this smoothie.

1½ cups unsweetened hemp milk

1 frozen medium banana

1 tbsp maple syrup

2 scoops pumpkin seed protein powder

1 In a blender, combine hemp milk, banana, maple syrup, and pumpkin seed protein powder. Blend on high speed until smooth.

2 Pour the mixture into two chilled glasses and serve immediately.

 **234 cals**

8g fat (0g saturated fat), 0mg cholesterol, 86mg sodium, 23g carbohydrates (14g sugar, 7g added sugar, 5g fiber), 22g protein

 5 min

 4 ingredients

Apricot Horchata With Cinnamon

This is a fresh spin on a classic, hacked by using rice flour instead of soaking dry grains overnight. Apricots, cinnamon, and a little honey add the perfect elements of sweetness.

2 cups low-fat milk

¼ cup rice flour

4 dried apricots

1 tsp cinnamon, plus extra for garnish

2 tsp honey

1 In a blender, combine milk, rice flour, apricots, cinnamon, honey, and as many ice cubes as needed. Blend on high speed until smooth.

2 Pour the mixture into two chilled glasses, sprinkle additional cinnamon on top, and serve immediately.

2g fat (2g saturated fat), 12mg cholesterol, 116mg sodium, 36g carbohydrates (19g sugar, 3g added sugar, 2g fiber), 9g protein

204 cals

5 min

5 ingredients

Cashews & Kale With Banana & Maple

Cashews make a creamy, dreamy smoothie—with no dairy in sight. Sip on a dose of greens and healthy fats in one drink— and you'll feel satisfied for hours.

½ cup raw cashews

1 frozen medium banana

1 cup chopped kale

1 tbsp maple syrup

1 Place cashews and 1 cup water in a small bowl and refrigerate for at least 4 hours or overnight. Drain before adding to the blender.

2 In a blender, combine soaked cashews, 1 cup fresh water, banana, kale, and maple syrup. Blend on high speed until smooth.

3 Pour the mixture into two chilled glasses and serve immediately.

16g fat (3g saturated fat), 0mg cholesterol, 25mg sodium, 34g carbohydrates (17g sugar, 7g added sugar, 4g fiber), 7g protein

 **292 cals**

 **5 min**

 4 ingredients

Turmeric Latte With Bananas & Maple

Turmeric is the spice that gives curry powder its golden color, but it's also a great addition to smoothies. The coconut milk enhances turmeric's anti-inflammatory properties.

1½ cups unsweetened plain or vanilla coconut milk beverage

1 tbsp maple syrup

2 frozen medium bananas

2 tsp ground turmeric

1 In a blender, combine coconut milk, maple syrup, bananas, turmeric, and black pepper to taste. Blend on high speed until smooth.

2 Pour the mixture into two chilled glasses, sprinkle a pinch of freshly ground black pepper on top, and serve immediately.

 **186 cals**

4g fat (3g saturated fat), 0mg cholesterol, 30mg sodium, 39g carbohydrates (22g sugar, 7g added sugar, 5g fiber), 2g protein

 **5 min**

 4 ingredients

Homemade Almond Milk With Bananas & Vanilla

You'll be amazed how scrumptious homemade almond milk can be. It's fresher, creamier, free of additives, and totally worth the extra time, especially for your taste buds.

1 cup raw almonds

2 medium frozen bananas

1 tsp pure vanilla extract

1 Place almonds and 1 cup water in a small bowl and refrigerate overnight. Drain before adding to the blender.

2 In a blender, combine almonds and 2 cups fresh water. Blend for 1 to 2 minutes and then strain through a fine mesh strainer lined with cheesecloth.

3 In a clean blender, combine strained almond milk, bananas, and vanilla extract. Blend on high speed until smooth.

4 Pour the mixture into two chilled glasses and serve immediately.

 **146 cals**

3g fat (0g saturated fat), 0mg cholesterol, 151mg sodium, 28g carbohydrates (15g sugar, 0g added sugar, 4g fiber), 2g protein

 **10 min**

 3 ingredients

Lentils & Peanut Butter With Banana

This smoothie is a peanut butter lover's dream! It gets an extra dose of plant-based potassium, iron, and fiber from the red lentils, which also have more protein than quinoa.

2 tbsp red lentils

¾ cup low-fat milk

2 tbsp natural peanut butter

1 frozen medium banana

1 Place red lentils and ½ cup water in a microwave-safe bowl. Cook on high until tender, about 2 to 4 minutes. Drain water and rinse lentils with fresh cold water to cool.

2 In a blender, combine lentils, milk, peanut butter, and banana. Blend on high speed until smooth.

3 Pour the mixture into two chilled glasses and serve immediately.

241 cals

10g fat (2g saturated fat), 4mg cholesterol, 66mg sodium, 26g carbohydrates (13g sugar, 0g added sugar, 5g fiber), 10g protein

10 min

4 ingredients

Creamy Cauliflower With Banana & Almond

This has the cancer-fighting benefits of cauliflower and the smoothness of heart-healthy almond butter. You won't taste much cauliflower, but you'd miss it if it wasn't there.

2 cups skim milk

1 cup frozen cauliflower florets

1 frozen medium banana

2 tbsp almond butter

1 In a blender, combine milk, cauliflower, banana, and almond butter. Blend on high speed until smooth.

2 Pour the mixture into two chilled glasses and serve immediately.

244 cals

9g fat (1g saturated fat), 5mg cholesterol, 120mg sodium, 31g carbohydrates (21g sugar, 0g added sugar, 4g fiber), 13g protein

5 min

4 ingredients

Dandy Watermelon With Apple

Dandelion greens are a seasonal treasure; look for them at your local farmers market. This combo of melon and greens contains 275% of your daily requirements for vitamin K.

1 cup 100% apple juice

2 cups diced fresh watermelon

1 cup chopped dandelion greens

1 In a blender, combine apple juice, watermelon, dandelion greens, and as many ice cubes as needed. Blend on high speed until smooth.

2 Pour the mixture into two chilled glasses and serve immediately.

0g fat (0g saturated fat), 0mg cholesterol, 32mg sodium, 28g carbohydrates (23g sugar, 0g added sugar, 2g fiber), 2g protein

 **113 cals**

 5 min

 3 ingredients

Carrots & Chai With Mango

If you're a fan of chai tea, this smoothie is a surefire winner. The cell-protecting benefits of the spices and tea–plus carrots and mango–make for a super nutrient-packed drink.

1 cup unsweetened almond milk

1 cup chilled brewed black tea

½ cup chopped carrots

1 cup frozen mango

1 tsp chai spice blend

1 In a blender, combine almond milk, tea, carrots, mango, and chai spice. Blend on high speed until smooth.

2 Pour the mixture into two chilled glasses and serve immediately.

86 cals

2g fat (0g saturated fat), 0mg cholesterol, 99mg sodium, 17g carbohydrates (13g sugar, 0g added sugar, 3g fiber), 2g protein

5 min

5 ingredients

Sweet Potato Shake With Orange & Ginger

Filled with vitamins A and C from the oranges and sweet potato, this tasty shake also has enough fiber to keep you feeling full and satisfied for hours after that first sip.

2 cups unsweetened almond milk

2 medium oranges, halved and juiced

1 cup cooked sweet potato

2 tsp freshly grated ginger

1 In a blender, combine almond milk, orange juice, sweet potato, ginger, and as many ice cubes as needed. Blend on high speed until smooth.

2 Pour the mixture into two chilled glasses, sprinkle a pinch of freshly ground black pepper on top, and serve immediately.

144 cals

3g fat (0g saturated fat), 0mg cholesterol, 101mg sodium, 29g carbohydrates (16g sugar, 0g added sugar, 6g fiber), 3g protein

10 min

4 ingredients

Vanilla Kefir With Lime

Kefir is a cultured milk beverage loaded with probiotics that promote healthy digestion. Blend with fresh lime and ice for a chilly, high-protein fermented beverage.

zest and juice of 2 limes

2 cups vanilla kefir

1 In a blender, combine lime zest and juice, kefir, and as many ice cubes as needed. Blend on high speed until smooth.

2 Pour the mixture into two chilled glasses and serve immediately.

 132 cals   3g fat (2g saturated fat), 10mg cholesterol, 126mg sodium, 15g carbohydrates (20g sugar, 8g added sugar, 3g fiber), 14g protein

 5 min

 2 ingredients

Celery & Cayenne With Lemon

This is a refreshing blend of celery and lemon with a kick of cayenne pepper. Sip on this smoothie between meals to curb cravings and to gain some extra daily nutrients.

1 cup chopped celery (stalks and leaves)

zest of 1 lemon

¼ tsp cayenne pepper

1 In a blender, combine 1 cup water, celery, lemon zest, cayenne, and as many ice cubes as needed. Blend on high speed until smooth.

2 Pour the mixture into two chilled glasses and serve immediately.

0g fat (0g saturated fat), 0mg cholesterol, 47mg sodium, 2g carbohydrates (1g sugar, 0g added sugar, 1g fiber), 0g protein

 **10 cals**

 5 min

 3 ingredients

Chocolate Cold Brew With Coffee & Mint

Start your day with this antioxidant-rich drink that's full of flavor but incredibly low in calories. Freeze leftover coffee in ice cube trays to make this smoothie as an afternoon pick-me-up.

2 cups chilled brewed coffee

1 cup low-fat milk

1 tbsp unsweetened cocoa powder

4 fresh mint leaves, plus extra for garnish

2 tsp granulated sugar

1 Pour coffee into ice cube trays and freeze for 4 hours or overnight.

2 In a blender, combine milk, coffee ice cubes, cocoa powder, mint, and sugar. Blend on high speed until smooth.

3 Pour the mixture into two chilled glasses, garnish with additional fresh mint leaves, and serve immediately.

 **81 cals**

2g fat (1g saturated fat), 5mg cholesterol, 70mg sodium, 12g carbohydrates (10g sugar, 4g added sugar, 1g fiber), 5g protein

 **5 min**

 5 ingredients

Spinach & Pears With Lemon

Spinach and pear should seem like a no-brainer pairing. Pears bring the filling fiber, while spinach offers vitamins and other nutrients to keep you strong to the finish.

1 cup skim milk

2 medium pears, Anjou or Bartlett varieties recommended, peeled, cored, and diced

2 cups raw baby spinach

1 tbsp freshly squeezed lemon juice

1 In a blender, combine milk, pears, spinach, lemon juice, and as many ice cubes as needed. Blend on high speed until smooth.

2 Pour the mixture into two chilled glasses and serve immediately.

 **131 cals**   1g fat (0g saturated fat), 3mg cholesterol, 77mg sodium, 29g carbohydrates (23g sugar, 0g added sugar, 5g fiber), 6g protein

 **5 min**

 4 ingredients

Coconut & Edamame With a Touch Of Honey

Edamame is one of a few plant-based foods that has many protein-building amino acids. Coconut and honey make this a perfectly balanced smoothie with all the macronutrients.

1½ cups unsweetened coconut milk beverage

1 cup frozen shelled edamame

1 tbsp honey

3 tbsp unsweetened shredded coconut

1 In a blender, combine coconut milk, edamame, honey, and shredded coconut. Blend on high speed until smooth.

2 Pour the mixture into two chilled glasses and serve immediately.

 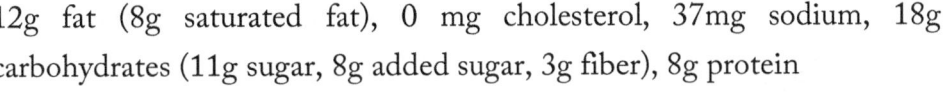

211 cals

12g fat (8g saturated fat), 0 mg cholesterol, 37mg sodium, 18g carbohydrates (11g sugar, 8g added sugar, 3g fiber), 8g protein

5 min

4 ingredients

Cucumber Chiller With Honeydew

This blend of cucumbers and juicy melon will help keep you hydrated and energized with plenty of vitamin C, B vitamins, and electrolytes–and a refreshing taste.

2 cups unsweetened almond milk

3 cups diced honeydew

1 medium cucumber, peeled, seeded, and chopped

6 fresh mint leaves

1 In a blender, combine almond milk, honeydew, cucumber, mint, and as many ice cubes as needed. Blend on high speed until smooth.

2 Pour the mixture into two chilled glasses and serve immediately.

 **145 cals** 3g fat (0g saturated fat), 0mg cholesterol, 109mg sodium, 30g carbohydrates (23g sugar, 0g added sugar, 4g fiber), 3g protein

 **5 min**

 4 ingredients

Fig & Almond Bowl With Bananas

This satisfying smoothie bowl contains no added sugar but does have an impressive 35% of your daily fiber needs. For best results, make sure the almond milk is ice-cold!

¾ cup vanilla almond milk

3 dried figs, roughly chopped

1 frozen medium banana

2 tbsp slivered almonds, for garnish

1 In a blender, combine almond milk, figs, and banana. Blend on high speed until smooth.

2 Pour the mixture into a medium bowl, sprinkle slivered almonds on top, and serve immediately.

 **289 cals**

9g fat (1g saturated fat), 0mg cholesterol, 94mg sodium, 49g carbohydrates (29g sugar, 0g added sugar, 9g fiber), 6g protein

 **5 min**

 4 ingredients

Plum & Jicama With Cashews & Honey

This smoothie contains no dairy but tastes like a milkshake thanks to blended cashews and jicama. Leave the plum skin on for more nutrients and an amazing lavender-colored drink.

¼ cup raw cashews

1 cup cashew or almond milk

1 plum, pitted and chopped

1 tbsp wildflower honey

¼ cup chopped jicama

1 Place cashews and 1 cup water in a small bowl and refrigerate for at least 4 hours or overnight. Drain before adding to the blender.

2 In a blender, combine soaked cashews, cashew milk, plum, honey, and jicama. Blend on high speed until smooth.

3 Pour the mixture into two chilled glasses and serve immediately.

169 cals

9g fat (2g saturated fat), 0mg cholesterol, 79mg sodium, 20g carbohydrates (13g sugar, 8g added sugar, 2g fiber), 3g protein

5 min

5 ingredients

Sweet Potato Bowl With Cantaloupe

This smoothie bowl is a great way to use a leftover baked sweet potato. The beta-carotene power will help protect skin and even make it glow.

½ cup unsweetened almond milk

1 cup cooked sweet potato

1½ cups finely chopped cantaloupe, divided

½ cup nonfat plain yogurt

1 In a blender, combine almond milk, sweet potato, 1 cup cantaloupe, yogurt, and as many ice cubes as needed. Blend on high speed until smooth.

2 Pour the mixture into a medium bowl, sprinkle the remaining cantaloupe on top, and serve immediately.

 **210 cals**

2g fat (0g saturated fat), 3mg cholesterol, 115mg sodium, 42g carbohydrates (26g sugar, 0g added sugar, 5g fiber), 9g protein

 10 min

 4 ingredients

Peachy Green Tea With Honey & Ginger

Frozen peaches blend beautifully, and because they're as nutritious as fresh, no need for peeling! Brewed tea offers a boost of flavor (and antioxidants) for no added calories.

1½ cups chilled brewed green tea

3 cups frozen peaches

¾ cup nonfat Greek yogurt

1 tbsp honey

1 tsp freshly grated ginger

1 In a blender, combine green tea, peaches, yogurt, honey, and ginger. Blend on high speed until smooth.

2 Pour the mixture into two chilled glasses and serve immediately.

 **153 cals**

0g fat (0g saturated fat), 0mg cholesterol, 32mg sodium, 33g carbohydrates (30g sugar, 8g added sugar, 3g fiber), 8g protein

 **10 min**

 5 ingredients

Virgin Bloody Mary With Celery & Lemon

Dress up low-sodium vegetable juice with a few simple ingredients. This low-carb beverage also features plenty of vitamins A, C, and K.

1 cup low-sodium vegetable juice

½ cup chopped celery

juice of ½ lemon

5 dashes of hot sauce (optional)

1 In a blender, combine vegetable juice, celery, lemon juice, hot sauce (if using), and as many ice cubes as needed. Blend on high speed until smooth.

2 Pour the mixture into two chilled glasses and serve immediately.

 **32 cals**

0g fat (0g saturated fat), 0mg cholesterol, 162mg sodium, 7g carbohydrates (5g sugar, 0g added sugar, 1g fiber), 1g protein

 **5 min**

 4 ingredients

Lemon & Beet With a Touch Of Honey

Because it's cool and refreshing and has the power of beets to help promote circulation and lower blood pressure, make this smoothie a part of your morning routine.

2 cups lemon seltzer

1 medium beet, peeled and chopped

1 tbsp honey

zest and juice of 1 lemon

1 In a blender, combine seltzer, beet, honey, lemon zest and juice, and as many ice cubes as needed. Blend on high speed until smooth.

2 Pour the mixture into two chilled glasses and serve immediately.

 **54 cals**   0g fat (0g saturated fat), 0mg cholesterol, 82mg sodium, 14g carbohydrates (12g sugar, 8g added sugar, 2g fiber), 1g protein

 5 min

 4 ingredients

Pumpkin & Maple With Banana & Cinnamon

Pumpkin spice latte lovers will swoon for this. Reserve leftover pumpkin purée in ice cube trays and add to the blender the next time you want to make this addictive smoothie.

¾ cup skim milk

1 tbsp maple syrup

¾ cup pumpkin purée

1 frozen medium banana

½ tsp ground cinnamon

1 In a blender, combine milk, maple syrup, pumpkin purée, banana, and cinnamon. Blend on high speed until smooth.

2 Pour the mixture into two chilled glasses and serve immediately.

141 cals

1g fat (0g saturated fat), 2mg cholesterol, 44mg sodium, 32g carbohydrates (22g sugar, 7g added sugar, 6g fiber), 5g protein

5 min

5 ingredients

PART 5: GREEN SMOOTHIES

Sweet Pea Shake With Pineapple & Lime

One of the best plant-based protein powders is made from peas. It has a mild flavor and blends beautifully, and most brands contain about 20 grams of protein per serving.

2 cups unsweetened coconut milk beverage

½ cup frozen peas

1 cup frozen pineapple

2 ounces unsweetened pea protein powder

zest and juice of 1 lime

1 In a blender, combine coconut milk, peas, pineapple, protein powder, and lime zest and juice. Blend on high speed until smooth.

2 Pour the mixture into two chilled glasses and serve immediately.

4g fat (4g saturated fat), 0mg cholesterol, 142mg sodium, 20g carbohydrates (11g sugar, 0g added sugar, 3g fiber), 22g protein

204 cals

5 min

5 ingredients

Spinach & Banana With Chia Seeds & Green Tea

Want to kickstart your day with a jolt of caffeine and a few healthy calories? This green drink has the ideal balance of healthy carbs, fat, and protein.

2 cups chilled brewed green tea

1 tbsp chia seeds

2 tbsp almond butter

1 frozen medium banana

1 cup baby spinach

1 In a blender, combine green tea, chia seeds, almond butter, banana, and spinach. Blend on high speed until smooth.

2 Pour the mixture into two chilled glasses and serve immediately.

177 cals

10g fat (1g saturated fat), 0mg cholesterol, 25mg sodium, 20g carbohydrates (8g sugar, 0g added sugar, 5g fiber), 6g protein

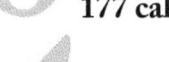

5 min

5 ingredients

Clementine & Banana With Wheatgrass & Coconut

Fresh wheatgrass can be hard to find, but wheatgrass powder is another way to take advantage of its antioxidant power. And a little goes a long way!

1½ cups coconut water

1 frozen medium banana

1 clementine

2 tsp wheatgrass powder

1 In a blender, combine coconut water, banana, clementine, and wheatgrass powder. Blend on high speed until smooth.

2 Pour the mixture into two chilled glasses and serve immediately.

 **111 cals**

 **5 min**

 4 ingredients

0g fat (0g saturated fat), 0mg cholesterol, 46mg sodium, 28g carbohydrates (17g sugar, 0g added sugar, 3g fiber), 2g protein

Matcha Latte With Banana & Honey

Matcha powder is finely ground green tea leaves, giving you nutrients and inflammation-fighting antioxidants. Research has also linked matcha to improved attention and memory.

1 cup unsweetened soy milk

½ cup chilled brewed green tea

2 tsp matcha powder

1 tbsp honey

1 frozen medium banana

1 In a blender, combine soy milk, green tea, matcha, honey, and banana. Blend on high speed until smooth.

2 Pour the mixture into two chilled glasses and serve immediately.

 **135 cals**

2g fat (0g saturated fat), 0mg cholesterol, 49mg sodium, 26g carbohydrates (17g sugar, 8g added sugar, 2g fiber), 4g protein

 5 min

 5 ingredients

Kale Lemonade With a Touch Of Honey

This low-calorie juice is a vitamin-filled complement to any meal–and without a lot of sugar. If you're not a fan of kale, its natural sweetness will pleasantly surprise you.

juice of 2 lemons

1 cup chopped kale

1 tbsp honey

1 In a blender, combine 2 cups water, lemon juice, kale, honey, and as many ice cubes as needed. Blend on high speed until smooth.

2 Pour the mixture into two chilled glasses and serve immediately.

 **55 cals**   0g fat (0g saturated fat), 0mg cholesterol, 13mg sodium, 14g carbohydrates (10g sugar, 8g added sugar, 1g fiber), 2g protein

 5 min

 3 ingredients

Avocado & Cilantro With a Splash Of Lime

This is a fresh green drink for when you aren't in the mood for something sweet. Enjoy this verdant and creamy smoothie with a light lunch.

2 cups coconut water

1 avocado

¼ cup fresh cilantro, leaves and stems

juice of ½ lime

1 In a blender, combine coconut water, avocado, cilantro, and as many ice cubes as needed. Blend on high speed until smooth.

2 Pour the mixture into two chilled glasses and serve immediately.

162 cals

11g fat (1g saturated fat), 0mg cholesterol, 66mg sodium, 20g carbohydrates (9g sugar, 0g added sugar, 6g fiber), 2g protein

5 min

4 ingredients

Key Lime & Romaine With Coconut & Banana

Lettuce in a smoothie? Heck yes! Romaine's mild freshness works beautifully with tangy key limes. Serve this smoothie over ice and start sipping your salad!

2 cups coconut water

juice of 2 key limes

1 cup chopped romaine lettuce

1 frozen medium banana

1 In a blender, combine coconut water, key lime juice, romaine lettuce, and banana. Blend on high speed until smooth.

2 Place ½ cup ice into two glasses, pour the mixture over the ice, and serve immediately.

0g fat (0g saturated fat), 0mg cholesterol, 63mg sodium, 35g carbohydrates (16g sugar, 0g added sugar, 5g fiber), 2g protein

 123 cals

 5 min

 4 ingredients

Ultimate Kombucha With Spinach

You'll be amazed how refreshing this green drink is. Combine a favorite kombucha along with some baby spinach and blend with ice for a frosty drink or blend and then pour over ice.

1½ cups kombucha

1 cup baby spinach

1 In a blender, combine kombucha, baby spinach, and as many ice cubes as needed. Blend on high speed until smooth.

2 Pour the mixture into two chilled glasses and serve immediately.

33 cals

5 min

2 ingredients

0g fat (0g saturated fat), 0mg cholesterol, 37 mg sodium, 7g carbohydrates (6g sugar, 0g added sugar, 1g fiber), 1g protein

Cucumber Shakeup With Lime

Use an English cucumber–which have smaller seeds than regular cucumbers–to maximize the nutrients in this refreshing drink. And leave the skin on for more minerals.

1 medium cucumber, diced

zest and juice of 1 lime

1 In a blender, combine 2 cups water, cucumber, lime zest and juice, and as many ice cubes as needed. Blend on high speed until smooth.

2 Pour the mixture into two chilled glasses and serve immediately.

 43 cals

 5 min

 2 ingredients

0g fat (0g saturated fat), 0mg cholesterol, 4mg sodium, 13g carbohydrates (4g sugar, 0g added sugar, 3g fiber), 1g protein

Kale & Green Apple With Ginger

Choose organic apples and leave the skin on to gain all the fiber apples offer. You don't have to limit this smoothie to just green apples. Use any type of apple—whatever's in season.

1½ cups unsweetened almond milk

2 cups chopped kale

2 medium green apples, cored and diced

1 tsp freshly grated ginger

1 In a blender, combine almond milk, kale, apples, ginger, and as many ice cubes as needed. Blend on high speed until smooth.

2 Pour the mixture into two chilled glasses and serve immediately.

2g fat (0g saturated fat), 0mg cholesterol, 165mg sodium, 41g carbohydrates (19g sugar, 0g added sugar, 8g fiber), 3g protein

 140 cals

 10 min

 4 ingredients

Tomatillo Whirl With Honey & Lime

There's more to tomatillos than making salsa! This tangy green drink is filling and offers many nutrients, like fiber, potassium, niacin, and iron—for about 40 calories per serving.

2 tomatillos, husks removed and flesh roughly chopped

1 tbsp honey

juice of 1 lime

1 In a blender, combine 1¼ cups water, tomatillos, honey, lime juice, as many ice cubes as needed, and sea salt to taste. Blend on high speed until smooth.

2 Pour the mixture into two chilled glasses and serve immediately.

0g fat (0g saturated fat), 0mg cholesterol, 0mg sodium, 11g carbohydrates (10g sugar, 8g added sugar, 1g fiber), 0g protein

 43 cals

 5 min

 3 ingredients

Mango Pops With Dates & Spinach

Who says you can't have popsicles for breakfast? These vitamin- and fiber-filled frozen treats are actually perfect for breakfast on a hot summer day.

1 cup unsweetened soy milk

1 cup frozen mango

2 pitted dates

1 cup baby spinach

½ cup granola

1 In a blender, combine soy milk, mango, dates, and spinach. Blend on high speed until smooth.

2 Pour the mixture into four popsicle molds and stir a little granola into each mold. Freeze for at least 4 hours before serving.

 **98 cals**

 10 min

 5 ingredients

2g fat (0g saturated fat), 0mg cholesterol, 58mg sodium, 19g carbohydrates (11g sugar, 4g added sugar, 3g fiber), 5g protein

Spinach & Bananas With Dates

Power up your day with this naturally sweetened green drink. This a great smoothie for those who want an introduction to a green drink–and this one has a lot of great flavor.

2 cups low-fat milk

2 medium bananas

2 large dates, pitted and chopped

1 cup baby spinach

1 In a blender, combine milk, bananas, dates, spinach, and as many ice cubes as needed. Blend on high speed until smooth.

2 Pour the mixture into two chilled glasses and serve immediately.

242 cals

3g fat (2g saturated fat), 10mg cholesterol, 153mg sodium, 46g carbohydrates (31g sugar, 0g added sugar, 6g fiber), 11g protein

5 min

4 ingredients

Avocado Bliss With Coconut & Banana

Nothing makes a green smoothie creamier than an avocado. Use an extra-ripe banana for just the right level of sweetness. This simple blend is filled with heart-healthy fats and fiber.

1½ cups unsweetened coconut milk beverage

1 avocado

1 frozen medium banana

1 In a blender, combine ½ cup water, coconut milk, avocado, and banana. Blend on high speed until smooth.

2 Pour the mixture into two chilled glasses and serve immediately.

200 cals

14g fat (4g saturated fat), 0mg cholesterol, 32mg sodium, 20g carbohydrates (8g sugar, 0g added sugar, 6g fiber), 2g protein

5 min

3 ingredients

Spinach & Apple With Broccoli & Banana

This smoothie will get your engine running with plenty of goodness from fruits and vegetables, including coconut water and banana teaming up for a potassium-loaded experience.

1 cup coconut water

½ cup broccoli

½ cup baby spinach

1 green apple, cored and chopped

1 medium banana

1 In a blender, combine coconut water, broccoli, spinach, apple, and banana. Blend on high speed until smooth.

2 Pour the mixture into two chilled glasses and serve immediately.

 **130 cals**   0g fat (0g saturated fat), 0mg cholesterol, 49mg sodium, 33g carbohydrates (21g sugar, 0g added sugar, 5g fiber), 2g protein

 **5 min**

 5 ingredients

Avocado & Kiwi With Mint

A few delicious green ingredients blended with coconut milk make this a vitamin-filled smoothie. Because it has 25% of your daily fiber, sip on this to keep you satisfied for hours.

1 cup unsweetened coconut milk beverage

1 avocado

1 kiwi

2 tbsp chopped fresh mint leaves

1 In a blender, combine coconut milk, avocado, kiwi, mint, and as many ice cubes as needed. Blend on high speed until smooth.

2 Pour the mixture into two chilled glasses and serve immediately.

 **157 cals**

13g fat (3g saturated fat), 0mg cholesterol, 24mg sodium, 11g carbohydrates (11g sugar, 0g added sugar, 6g fiber), 2g protein

 **5 min**

 4 ingredients

Pineapple & Parsley With Spinach & Banana

Stop thinking about parsley as a garnish. It's actually a nutrient powerhouse. This herb boasts vitamins A, C, and K as well as minerals, like potassium, iron, and calcium.

2¼ cups coconut water

2 cups frozen pineapple

¼ cup roughly chopped parsley

2 cups baby spinach

1 medium frozen banana

1 In a blender, combine coconut water, pineapple, parsley, spinach, and banana. Blend on high speed until smooth.

2 Pour the mixture into two chilled glasses and serve immediately.

 **178 cals** 1g fat (0g saturated fat), 0mg cholesterol, 77mg sodium, 44g carbohydrates (33g sugar, 0g added sugar, 4g fiber), 3g protein

 **5 min**

 5 ingredients

Ginger Detox With Pineapple

Detoxify the natural way with this blend of tummy-pleasing ginger and inflammation-fighting pineapple. This combo will also help promote a glowing complexion.

1½ cups unsweetened almond milk

juice of 1 lemon

1½ cups frozen pineapple

2 tsp freshly grated ginger

1 In a blender, combine almond milk, lemon juice, pineapple, and ginger. Blend on high speed until smooth.

2 Pour the mixture into two chilled glasses and serve immediately.

 95 cals

3g fat (0g saturated fat), 0mg cholesterol, 82mg sodium, 18g carbohydrates (11g sugar, 0g added sugar, 3g fiber), 2g protein

 5 min

 4 ingredients

Zucchini Blast With Bok Choy & Lemon

This is a savory burst of green goodness to help curb cravings between meals. Bok choy is a mild Chinese cabbage that in this smoothie provides just the right amount of bite.

½ zucchini

1 small head baby bok choy, trimmed and roughly chopped

juice of 1 lemon

1 In a blender, combine 1 cup water, zucchini, bok choy, lemon juice, and as many ice cubes as needed. Blend on high speed until smooth.

2 Pour the mixture into two chilled glasses and serve immediately.

0g fat (0g saturated fat), 0mg cholesterol, 32mg sodium, 4g carbohydrates (2g sugar, 0g added sugar, 1g fiber), 1g protein

17 cals

5 min

3 ingredients

Kale Chiller With Lemon

Coconut-flavored Greek yogurt and protein powder team up with kale and lemon for a green smoothie that's ideal for any health-conscious sipper. It will tempt all your taste buds!

1 cup chopped kale

¾ cup nonfat coconut Greek yogurt

1 scoop protein powder

zest and juice of 1 lemon

1 In a blender, combine 1½ cups water, kale, yogurt, protein powder, and lemon zest and juice. Blend on high speed until smooth.

2 Pour the mixture into two chilled glasses and serve immediately.

148 cals

4g fat (2g saturated fat), 8mg cholesterol, 113mg sodium, 14g carbohydrates (8g sugar, 4g added sugar, 1g fiber), 15g protein

5 min

4 ingredients